A More Perfect Union

Book One

(a primer on governance)

by Ergo (the Martian)

printed in the United States of America

First Edition

ISBN-13: 978-1517755164
ISBN-10: 1517755166

Printed in the United States of America by:
CreateSpace

This book is dedicated to Homo Sapiens everywhere and their never-ending quest for betterment.

Table of Contents

PROLOGUE:

'"Contrary to modernization theory's progressive assumptions, there was no reason to assume that political development was any more likely than political decay. Political order emerges as a result of the achievement of some equilibrium among the contending forces within society. But as time goes on, change occurs internally and externally: the actors who established the original equilibrium themselves evolve or disappear, new actors appear... As a result, the preceding equilibrium no longer holds and political decay results until existing actors come up with a new set of rules and institutions to restore order."

Samuel Huntington
Political Order in Changing Societies"

"... the United States has long-standing and powerful institutions, but they have been subject to political decay. Government institutions that are supposed to serve public purposes have been captured by powerful private interests, such that democratic majorities have a difficult time asserting their control. The problem is not just one of money and power it also has to do with rigidities of the rules themselves and of the ideas supporting them."

Francis Fukuyama
"Political Order And Political Decay"

Why have I written this book? Because I am concerned about how our political and social polarization is stifling our national ability to find common ground and achieve a consensus on what is in our collective best interest. All too often our national leaders view these issues as zero sum games where "my way or the highway" is the prevailing theme and compromise is viewed as weakness and a betrayal of our beliefs. As a counter to this, this primer will strive to determine why this is and once we understand that, to ascertain the truth and facts pertaining to these issues and to establish a sound foundation on which to develop viable solutions. If we can draw conclusions grounded on reasoned analysis and clearly and fairly state the underlying facts, we can devise workable solutions. I still believe we are a great nation. Greater than any nation in history. But I also believe we could have achieved more and as importantly that we can do better. Our nation, in the end, is the sum of its people and each of the more than 300 million of us is as unique as our DNA. How we reconcile and harness our individual goals and desires defines us. This inner struggle, the friction it creates and the heat it generates is the force driving us constantly to evaluate and reinvent ourselves and our nation. This process has driven us at times to do some truly great things and at times to do things we would rather forget. As such, the path of our democracy has not been a straight line but more like an undulating sound wave with hills and valleys, but the long term trend line has been straight, true and rising.

Unfortunately, we are now in one of our valleys and our trend line is becoming flat. We are near a tipping point - our "current political equilibrium" no longer holds - in short, we are losing our way. Our political and social structures have slipped into division and our leaders and decision makers are failing to lead. Their pronouncements are more often purposely misleading, full of misrepresentations and unverified suppositions that cloud and distort reality. As a nation, we are becoming increasingly polarized. Listening only to the voices we want to hear and drowning out those we don't. Mainstream media is losing its audience to the fringe, both left and right. Much of what passes for thoughtful analysis and discussion is, in reality, merely bias attempts to justify and frame the arguments to conform to fixed preordained agendas. That our elected representatives have lost their ability to deal with our problems is clearly evident. We have five percent of the world's population yet we incarcerate twenty-five percent of the world's inmates. We spend forty-three percent of the world's expenditures on defense while 47 million of us are on "food stamps" and 22% of our children are living in poverty. Our health care costs are eighteen percent of GDP while on average the other OECD (Organization for Economic Co-operation and Development) countries are only spending about nine percent or less. Are we really any safer, healthier or happier than the rest of these countries? I doubt it.

So how did this happen and how did we get this way? It is not that we, as a people, lack reason, purpose or good intent. The primary cause is that our governmental structure no longer fits our societal or cultural needs and as a result our governance is failing us. As a society we have evolved but our historically authoritarian top down elitist and establishment governance model has not. This, in turn, has led to our governance being distorted by the forces of "special interests". Our elected representatives collectively approach our problems with predetermined solutions that support these "special interests" agendas and then work backwards to fashion a basis (often fictional) to justify them. Even when the facts are clear and undisputed, policies are often filtered through the lens of their own political perspective whether it be liberal, conservative or somewhere in between - and rendered in the service of their constituents which, incidentally, are not "we the people" who elected them but the "special interests" who finance, support and direct them. While these representatives do, where possible, support their constituents social and political philosophies they do so only to the extent that those interests are not in conflict with the "special interests" they are beholden to. This goes a long way to explain why Congress is flirting with a single digit approval rating. Unfortunately, the polling organizations are asking the wrong constituency - if they asked the "special interests" they would find that Congress is batting a thousand.

While these comments may seem overly strident one need look no further than the debate regarding global warming for vindication. Here the "special interests" are big oil and energy with a supporting cast of major industrial firms that are heavy carbon consumers. One of their strongest supporters is Texas Governor Rick Perry. Both in his book and during his previous presidential campaign debates he claimed that global warming does not exist and further says that the vast majority of climatic scientist agree with him. This is a purposeful distortion of facts and 180 degrees from the reality. Since World War II the international merchant marine has continually recorded ocean temperatures world wide. What they have found is an uneven but steady increase in the oceans temperatures. The Arctic Sea is now melting annually to the point where a Northwest Passage actually exists and in a few years Glacier National Park will be glacier free. The reality is that global warming is a documented fact and contrary to the Governor's assertion the vast majority of climate scientists agree with this fact. On May 1, 2012 the New York Times reported that 97% of working climatologists believe in global warming. Since then the Wall Street Journal reported, on

March 8,2013, that scientists have verified the earth has warmed as much in the past 100 years as it has in the preceding 11,300 years. More recently a committee of the world's concerned scientists stated that they are 95% certain that global warming is the product of human kind. Yet here "special interests" insist that this is not so and our elected representatives react accordingly. And the beat goes on. The 2016 presidential candidate, Senator Ted Cruz, claims that climate change advocates are "flat earthers" and his fellow senator Jim Inhofe continually calls Global Warming the "greatest hoax ever perpetrated on the American people". They are both wrong and I suspect they know it - but global warming is not something that the big oil and energy "special interests" want debated.

In this case reality can easily be found in concrete facts. But not all issues can be substantiated and fact checked or empirically distilled from raw data. Many issues including ones like the need or value of a national healthcare system require analyses from a more nuanced perspective. While the current healthcare debate over Obamacare centers on claims from the left that the law does not provide enough protection against large insurance companies and from the right that it is too expensive and an intrusion on our privacy it fails to address the more fundamental question of - "what is the proper role of an economically developed democracy in the 21st century regarding the health and wellbeing of its citizens?". And in that context "why are 33 million Americans still without healthcare insurance?" Answering these questions is a prerequisite to any debate on the specifics on the merits of the law itself.

But this debate is being misrepresented and compromised by "special interests". So before we can move on and accurately assess the law's merits we need to remove the distorting effects of "special interests" and that can only happen with a fundamental change in our governmental structure. To accomplish this we will need to understand both where we came from and how we got to where we are now. This is where it gets dicey because historical perspective is subjective, and like beauty, is in the eye of the beholder. However, I will endeavor to expunge and inhibit my bias from this process and strive be factually objective. To that end, it would help if I could think of myself as a newly arrived Martian observer, free from past earthly experiences and starting this process with a blank slate and observing reality from the 50,000 foot level.

From this detached solar vantage point I could reason that the government of 1790 or even 1900 would not have needed a national healthcare policy. Back then, America was still mostly agrarian and healthcare was the province of solo medical practitioners - one-on-one with their patients. But this is 2015, and less than 2% of Americans live on farms. We are a far more integrated and interdependent society with vast medical complexes and legions of specialists covering every medical discipline and serving large regional populations. The solo practitioner is an endangered species. Because of this, a cohesive national healthcare strategy is certainly a legitimate function of our national government. This does not mean Obamacare is the right solution. It just frames the debate away from the good, bad and ugly of Obamacare to one of governmental purpose and responsibility in today's complex society. The reality is that securing the health and wellbeing of our citizens is just as important a governmental purpose as regulating commerce or providing for its national defense and is something every other economically advanced democracy (OECD members) have already accomplished. Whether Obamacare is the best approach to achieving this goal is an entirely different question - one I will address in a later volume, but for now I will continue my approach and keep thinking like a Martian while leaving it to you to judge the soundness and reality of my ensuing observations, arguments and proposals.

Ergo (The Martian)
Somewhere in America
October, 2015

INTRODUCTION:

As I stated in the Prologue, much of what today passes as factually based and reasoned discussion is actually a process anchored in fantasies and preconceived "special interests" agendas that distort reality solely for that purpose. My purpose here is twofold. The first is to explore why our governmental structure no longer serves our evolving needs and to offer solutions. The second is to both expose these myths and to identify the reality underlying our social, political, financial and environmental issues and based on this reality, to propose meaningful and doable solutions to resolve them.

But first we must explore why our governmental structure is not working. I purposely focus on "special interests" as the proximate cause of this and our current political gridlock, not because "special interests", as a group, are composed of bad or immoral people. They are not - at bottom they are us. We are all, by virtue of being citizens and voters in one way or another "special interests". The difference between what I am labeling as "special interests" and the citizen voter is that the citizen voter is local and only has influence in the district where he or she is domiciled and exerts influence on his or her elected officials in equal proportion to all other voters in their district. Whereas the "special interests" I am referring to are cross-border actors that exert undue influence on elected officials universally through the exercise of their enormous financial resources. While I believe they often put their own interest before those of their country I also believe their actions are not conspiratorial and each seeks to promote his or her own personal interests. Some may be plainly selfish and others may believe in what they are doing and that they have every right to do so. However, the fact remains that a Sheldon Adelman injecting twenty million dollars into the political process exerts vastly more influence than a Sheldon Adelman citizen voter and this distorts and corrupts the political process regardless of what his motivation or intent rnay be. The issue then is how to re-balance our diverse political forces to re-establish political equilibrium. But there is another less obvious cause to our current political morass and that is that our existing authoritarian, establishment, elitist and top down governmental structure no longer fits or is capable of solving our societal needs and this is our primary problem and it is also why "special interests" exist.

As things stand now, our democratic equilibrium is out of balance to the point where "special interests" have gained the high ground. Democracy works best and serves the greater good when its various constituencies have a balance of power. When the interests of business, labor, agriculture, urban, rural and cultural are balanced against each other compromise is inevitable. Today, that balance has been distorted due to the financial dependence of our elected officials on campaign contributions from "special interests". They are now dominating the playing field because that is where the money is and let's not forget that "money is the mother's milk of politics". No congressman or senator can be elected solely on the contributions of his or her constituents. "Special interest" financial support is indispensable and it is provided not because "special interests" are egalitarian but because they are looking for a return on their investment. The result is that we are, as a nation, becoming more extractive and less inclusive. We are now governed by the Golden Rule, which postulates that "he who has the gold makes the rules". Where the benefits of our national efforts are being unfairly garnered by the few at the expense of the many.

This is not irresolvable. But significant change will require an organized effort from outside the existing political framework to recast balance, level the playing field and create a new equilibrium between the various social and political forces that compete for governmental power. One that allows us to achieve a democracy that is more inclusive and balanced. Where the voices of all can be heard and our national treasure can be more equally shared.

The solutions I am proposing fall into two categories. The first, this book, will focus on structural changes that, in some cases, will require constitutional amendments. These changes will re-establish democratic equilibrium, strengthen our democracy, expand constitutional protections and reflect the political reality of the 21st century. At the very least this will mean a complete change in how elections are financed to eliminate the undue influence of "special interests". The second part, which I will offer in a separate volume, is procedural. Aimed at how a more balanced and representative Congress can improve the functions of government and reverse "special interest" influence that permeates so much of our current law. A Congress that is truly the voice of the people would never have enacted legislation exempting Big Pharma from negotiating drug prices with Medicare. But one beholden to "special interests" certainly had no problem doing so,

However, reforming our governmental structure comes first and is an absolute and necessary prerequisite to any possible improvement in our governance. But before we can discuss structural reform we need to take a step back and look at how our democracy and governmental structure developed. Once we understand that we can move on to the question that is at the heart of our democratic discourse. And that is - "what is the function and purpose of government in the twenty-first century, and how can we achieve it?"

.

1. - Historical Perspective:

As a nation, our democratic roots go back almost a millennium to feudal England and a process that began with the Magna Carta. By the time of North American colonization, in the early seventeenth century, England had already taken the first embryonic and tentative steps toward democracy. While the country was still very much a monarchy and the King still supreme, Parliament was gaining power and relevance through its representation of the nation's various political factions. A century on, England had made the leap, through The Glorious Revolution, into a functioning constitutional monarchy (although it lacked a written constitution). Its legal system (common law) had developed to a point where substantial individual rights and protections were in place, and the various national actors - Crown, lords, farmers, merchants, artisans, manufacturers, clergy and professionals were now sufficiently balanced. This political development was also mirrored in the thirteen colonies where by 1770 each had developed similar democratic processes even though they remained first and foremost subordinate to England and the Crown. However, this was changing.

To this point, the vast majority of colonials were loyal British subjects and whatever their problems with England they were perceived as primarily issues with Parliament and not wlth the king. King George lll was still revered as a benevolent benefactor and loyal friend to the colonies. However, various acts of Parliament, such as the Stamp Act, had begun to alienate merchants and other segments of society. When attempts at reconciliation and compromise failed, the seeds of discontent were irrevocably sown. Minor hostilities simmered and then erupted into armed insurrection and support for the Crown eroded. By 1776 a majority of colonists had changed their allegiance and concluded that independence was now their only option.

At the onset of all-out war the colonists quickly recognized their need to ban together for both their common defense and to secure independence. As Benjamin Franklin is said to have quipped "we must all hang together or assuredly we shall all hang separately". Though each colony viewed itself as a sovereign and independent state their common needs led to the formation of the Continental Congress and the establishment of a Continental Army. After six years of dogged perseverance and military support from France, independence was finally achieved in 1781. Looking back on this era it seems truly amazing that in a little more than a decade these thirteen loyal English colonies had morphed into an independent fledgling nation. Awed by what they had accomplished and concerned but confident about their future. They now faced the daunting task of defining their new nationhood. However, on closer inspection, what was accomplished is not so surprising. From a political perspective the revolution changed little. Before and after the rule of law and representative government were the norm and firmly established and local politics had changed little. What the revolution did change was an overriding sense of being part of a nation - The British nation. As they looked around they saw themselves as 13 independent states loosely bound together by their common history and recent struggles but not yet quite a nation. At the same time it was also apparent that there was a continuing need for some form of unifying government if for no other reason than for their common defense.

While their options were several they essentially boiled down to two separate and competing philosophical views of government. One was that a strong central government was essential to preserve their new-found freedoms. This was the position of the Federalists championed by Alexander Hamilton. The other was that such a government would eventually evolve into another monarchy and therefore a central government must remain weak and kept in check. This was the view of the Republicans and its leader Thomas Jefferson. In 1781 this fear of monarchy was also the view of the majority of the people. While they were no longer colonists and subjects of the king they were not yet fully Americans either. They were somewhere in between. Each viewed his or her primary allegiance to their state (i,e., a Virginian, a New Yorker, etc.) with regional affiliation close behind (i.e.Northerner, Southerner or Westerner). Being an American was thought of more as a geographic rather than political designation. So it is not surprising that their solution, the Articles of Confederation (Articles), were adopted as a tentative and cautious step toward nationhood - one where political power firmly resided with each of the several states.

However, from day one, the Articles, proved an inadequate solution for nationhood. The very restrictions that kept them weak also kept them ineffective. They provided for a common defense and granted Congress the right to do so but they failed to provide any funding other than voluntary state grants. Congress could request these funds but it could not compel them. Nor did it have any authority to settle claims that arose between states, or create an independent national judiciary to resolve these issues.

Congress was effectively, little more than a national debating society with the power of persuasion but not enforcement. While it is not entirely analogous, the European Union suffers from some of these same issues and limitations - especially in the regulation of its finances and the Euro. And if the EU constituent countries fail to grant more national sovereignty to a central government it may suffer the same fate and for the same reason - failure to face or understand reality.

To that extent, the Articles represent an early example of perception over reality. The majority of citizens inclined toward the Jeffersonian philosophy that a central government was a necessary evil - one to be tolerated and embraced but only to the extent that it was absolutely necessary. What they failed to recognize was that their political needs had moved beyond the capabilities of a loosely defined confederation. Through the growing complexity of territorial, political, defense and interstate trade issues they had already become a de facto country requiring a real and effective federal government. And the reality of this weakness very soon became apparent.

By 1787, just six years into the Articles, efforts were already under way to fix them. What originated as a localized conference to solve a Potomac River navigation dispute between Virginia and Maryland grew into a national convention to address more substantive changes to the Articles. But as the delegates worked through the Articles' deficiencies it quickly became apparent that a replacement, not a revision, was the only solution. What transpired that summer was truly miraculous. Especially when considered in the light of the results that could have occurred given the available options. By comparison the Congress of 1776 faced a more narrow and focused dilemma, and while breaking from England was certainly a courageous and death-defying act it was also a clear-cut decision. The colonies either remained British and found solutions to their problems or they made a complete break. There were no half measures. But for the Congress of 1787 the outcome was anything but obvious. Their options were varied and the obstacles to agreement daunting. Besides the issue of what form of union to propose, failure to compromise on regional issues could have resulted in the formation of several regional countries, i.e. a Southern Confederacy, a Northern Confederacy and possibly another emerging political entity west of the Alleghenys. Through some combination of political evolution, innovation and inspiration what emerged that summer was an imaginative and visionary blueprint for governance - the Constitution. One that has endured for more than 200 years. The genius of this document is its plasticity. It laid out form and function but not specificity. But that does not mean that It is amorphous. There are limits placed on the various governmental departments - the executive, legislative and judicial, that outline their functions and with enough clarity to define their roles yet with enough flexibility to remain relevant in the ensuing years as the nation was transformed through social, political and technical evolution from a rural agrarian society into a highly commercialized urban industrial one as the small hamlets and villages of 1787 gave way to urban metropolises where the majority now live. Yet, while this was a bold step forward and a radical departure from monarchical rule it did so by adopting much of the authoritarian, establishment, elitist and top down governmental structure of the one it was replacing. The fundamental differences being that Britain had a hereditary monarch were we had an elected President (first magistrate); they had a hereditary House of Lords where we had an elected Senate (although neither the President nor the Senate were elected directly). And there were similarities as well - they had an elected House of Commons and we had an elected House of Representatives (however, in both cases the franchise was very limited) and their judiciary like ours was a separate and independent department. In retrospect this was not at all surprising given the dearth of democratic models available to chose from. Over the last two centuries we have continually improved on this model but we are now left with one that is out of focus and functionally no longer fits our societal needs.

Fortunately, the Constitution's enduring adaptability provides an avenue for relief. Our founders were sufficiently farsighted to include a mechanism for modification as future circumstances required. The ability to amend the Constitution has kept it fresh and relevant throughout its course. Slavery, which was the third rail of colonial politics, was subsequently abolished through Constitutional amendment after the Civil War. An issue that would have rendered the nation still born in 1787 and almost destroying it seventy years later was resolved as were the issues of direct election of senators and women's suffrage. This adaptability allows the Constitution to reflect both societal changes and new political realities. As such, the Constitution remains today, a work in progress.

The Constitution's other enduring attribute was its method of adoption. By requiring that the citizens of the several states ratify the Constitution directly rather than through state legislatures, the Constitution created a federal government of the people and not of the states. This distinction has been at the heart of most constitutional controversies ever since and is still a central focus of party politics today. And is just one aspect of the inability of either party to gain a clear vision of where the nation is or how it should be governed.

We are now mired between competing political philosophies - neither of which recognizes the economic, societal or geopolitical reality of today, with each paying homage to the past, i.e. an America that no longer exists. And as Martin Wolfe (chief economics commentator for The Financial Times, London) has keenly observed, "the past is a foreign country". For Democrats, that past is somewhere around 1932 - 1952,the era of the New Deal. For Republicans, it is more distant, closer to 1890 - 1910. With both political philosophies rooted in the 200 year-old unresolved issue of Federalism versus "States Rights". Which in reality is a proxy for the current debate over "Big Government" versus "Small Government". This results in a distorted view of reality: producing governmental policies that are overlapping, inadequate and ineffective. The amount of waste created because of duplicate federal and state agencies is staggering. To illustrate this point we need look no further than how government handles the issue of Unemployment Insurance. Prior to the New Deal unemployment insurance was not considered an obligation or purpose of government - neither state nor federal. However, when the Great Depression set in and the unemployment rate climbed to 25%, that thinking changed. For Congress the solution to this problem was legislation providing for a federally funded unemployment insurance program - but one that was administered solely by the states. At the time this solution was a satisfactory accommodation of the various political factions needed to pass Congress. It no longer is and has since morphed into a patchwork of inconsistent state programs with varying criteria for tax rates, eligibility, benefits and their duration. This unnecessarily creates excess administrative costs and fails to provide an equitable solution for what is today, a national problem.

From its inception, this legislation was hampered by the southern politics of Jim Crow, racism and segregation. The political reality of the time was that southern Democrats would not sign on to any legislation that would undercut their control of segregationist policies so any federally administered program was out of the question. Additionally, business and labor were more localized so a state-oriented program was not a major detriment and it was also a nod to "states rights". While it was essentially a big government program its shared responsibility kept states in the game.

Fast forward to today and the economic landscape is vastly different and comparatively almost unrecognizable. Our twenty-first century economy is not only more diverse, it is global and labor moves with it. The federal government still financially subsidizes the program but the majority of funding is now provided by state unemployment taxes, This leads to an uneven result where states with high unemployment have the least funding to provide for benefits while states with low unemployment are over funded. Nevada and North Dakota are prime examples. Besides this inequity, state-based unemployment systems extract a heavy toll on business. Any firm with national reach has to file quarterly returns in all fifty states. These returns are not uniform and each state has established its own reporting criteria which makes compliance more difficult. This also creates an enormous overlap of administrative cost for both the private sector and the states. A reordering of this system as a federally funded but privately administered program would eliminate much of thls overlapping cost, yielding a more uniform and equitable benefit program and one that is more responsive to the needs of today's mobile workforce (more on this in Book 2 - especially the privately administered part).

This represents just one small example of the bloated, inefficient and expensive duplication that is currently emblematic of state and federal governance. And Illustrates the fallacy and myth of dual federal and state sovereignty and shows how our leaders are mired in the past, out of touch and rear facing - like generals fighting the last war.

1.2 - The Road Forward:

To resolve this, we need not be visionary as much as realistic and pragmatic. Our governmental dysfunction belies the fact that in the past two hundred plus years America has grown from a loose collection of British Colonies into a world leading and powerful democracy. Our financial and military prowess are beyond match. We have accomplished this seemingly impossible feat in spite of, not because of, our self-imposed social and political obstructions. What we need now is a course correction and a new national vision based on the realization of where we are - not where we have been. To chart this course we must first define the purpose of our democratic governance in what is today a multicultural, industrialized, pluralistic and increasingly global world. And secondly, to clearly state how this definition should be implemented. In answer, I have staked out solutions that are based on what I perceive are solid empirical facts. Others may have differing opinions and answers to these questions, but however they are resolved the solutions must be solidly based on factual reality and not fantasy, prejudice, supposition or conjecture.

With this in mind, let's move on to the first issue. The short answer to which is that the purpose of government is to provide for the well being, betterment and common defense of its citizens and it exists solely to serve these ends and no others. Government is not something separate from the people, it is the people - *we the people*.

Defining how this is determined and what it means depends on a number of variables and viewpoints: namely, our societal needs, our political and governmental philosophy, and our functional resource capabilities. At our nation's inception, we had neither the political desire nor the perceived need to provide a social safety net and we certainly lacked the governmental infrastructure or resources to provide for one. People were largely self-sufficient and they viewed themselves as such. They farmed, fished or hunted for food, built their own houses and made their own clothes. Governmental purpose was functionally limited to providing for public safety and civil order. By 1900 our functional and resource capabilities had evolved to the point where government could provide for this but societal and political will were lacking. At the time, the concepts of unemployment insurance, social security or universal health care were viewed by most as radical socialism.

Today these concepts are mainstream and the current debate is not whether government should provide them but only to what extent, how and for whom. This debate is framed in turn by the tenets of our various political philosophies - primarily Democrat, Republican and Libertarian - all of which are missing the point, anchored in the past and channeled by our existing governmental structure. Each issue has predetermined solutions predicated on their partisan views which are skewed by political philosophy and supported by questionable or factious facts. This is, at best, circular thinking. As the late Senator Daniel Patrick Moynihan said "each of us are entitled to our own opinion but not our own facts". If we are to improve our societal and governmental functions we will have to re-think these issues. And to do that we have to free ourselves of our past biases and prejudices. If we can do that, we can achieve a new political paradigm and a clearer understanding of our evolving sense of government and its purpose - one based on factual reality.

Our concepts of democracy, politics and govemment have changed greatly over the last two centuries. They are still evolving and will continue to do so but the trend line is clear. That trend is toward a more inclusive and expansive democracy. Winston Churchill's observation that - democracy is not the best form of government but clearly better than any of the alternatives - still holds. However, It should not be viewed as an impediment to attempts to improve it. We have made great strides over the course of our brief history. We began as a nation of European (mostly British), Native and African peoples. But it was the Europeans who were dominant and while the Declaration of Independence said all men are created equal it meant only white European men. Thls is no longer the case. Slavery has been abolished and universal suffrage achieved so there is much to be proud of but still more to do. Levels of social and political inequity and economic inequality still prevail. To paraphrase George Orwell - we are all equal, but some of us are more equal than others. Resolving this imbalance and making our democracy and governance more inclusive is the task at hand and one that is consistent with our social and political evolution.

Metaphorically we can think of this process as a national journey - a road kip. We may not be certain of where we are going but we know it is out there in front of us. As a people we are always moving forward, never stopping, passing social and political milestone after milestone in our national quest. Any observation of where we are is only a fleeting snapshot soon to be history. While our journey is forward and expansive it is also restricted and limited by the boundaries of the Constitution. When in the past we have hit these boundaries we have had to either change course or change the constitutional boundaries - something we have already accomplished 27 times. We are again approaching these boundaries and we are again faced with the choice of changing the boundaries or changing our course. What I am proposing will require a little of both. But this is not so much a new course as it is a continuation of the trajectory we have been on for the past two centuries. I am proposing a political philosophy that is very much centered on the spirit, vision and ideals of our founding fathers but updated to reflect today's reality. How this has been interpreted and applied, over time, has varied but the spirit of these ideals have always been at the center of our journey. Namely, a democracy that is expansive and inclusive. At times we have veered toward socialism, liberalism, conservatism and populism but at center our political philosophy has always been what I call Americanism and it is the foundation on which I stake out my view of the future. This view may be seen by some as radically different than today's mainstream political philosophies but I think it is actually the opposite and it is the dysfunctional polarization of today's politics that is out of focus.

My definition of the role of government and its purpose - to provide for the betterment and well being of its citizens is equally dependent on societal and political will and governmental resource capability. In 1790 governmental resource capability was lacking regardless of whether it was desired or needed. Today, the situation is different. We are the world's richest nation and it would be difficult to overstate the success we have achieved. What has changed and what today's politics is missing is that we are no longer individually self-sufficient. Regardless of our station in life we are now all part of a totally integrated and interdependent society. None of us can exist without the support of others. Yet, in many ways we still see ourselves, not as a whole, but as divided into different factions and groups - viewing democracy as a zero sum game where any advantage to one is a detriment to the other. You can see this thinking reflected in how we view ourselves. We call ourselves African-Americans, Italian-Americans, Chinese-Americans and Native-Americans - but not Americans of African, Italian, Chinese or Native extraction. This then is polarizing and false thinking. We are one nation and we are all first and foremost Americans. This thinking also belies the reality that the betterment of one results in the betterment of us all. The reality is - we may have come here on different boats and at different times but we are now all together in the same boat. Viewed from this perspective I believe the purpose and responsibility of our twenty-first century government is to provide for a more expansive social safety net - one that both fulfills the spirit of individual equality and in doing so better serves our national purpose. In this way we can become more egalitarian in our governmental function and by extension achieve a more expansive and inclusive democracy - and one that is also more prosperous.

1.3 - Americanism Rejuvenated:

Specifically, I believe that government is responsible for providing each of us with a guaranteed minimum standard of living. One that includes adequate sustenance, shelter, health care, educational opportunities and financial security. No American should go to bed hungry, live in squalor, lack medical treatment, be limited or deprived of educational opportunity or be financially insecure. There are qualifications to this guarantee and each of us has responsibility to safeguard this promise, but for the vast majority of Americans this is a promise that is at the heart of governmental purpose and our national betterment - and it is one that needs to be kept.

This may sound like old style socialism but it is anything but. What I envision is a government with a substantially smaller footprint, more market oriented and one clearly and robustly committed to our societal needs. Nor is providing for this simply a matter of raising taxes and spending more money. Stripped of bloat, duplication and bureaucratic waste there are more than ample resources for this purpose. This is simply a matter of being smarter and more focused on our societal needs and applying our resources more soundly. Our government, in theory, is already providing most of what I outlined. It provides food stamps (Supplemental Nutritional Assistance Program), Section 8 housing vouchers, Medicare and Medicaid, Aid to Dependent Children, disability, workmen's compensation and unemployment insurance, minimum wages, Social Security, Pell Grants plus numerous other assistance programs. Taken in sum, these programs would appear to provide a robust social safety net but in actuality they are porous, overlapping, bloated, and wasteful. On closer inspection and in spite of all this government largess there are still large sections of our population that are hurting with one in seven Americans living below the poverty line. Thirty-four percent of New York City homeless shelter residents hold full time jobs. Most students graduating from college carry a heavy burden of student loans. The total student loans outstanding are now over one point two trillion dollars with the average student carrying a balance in excess of $35,000. Healthcare is still a major issue and not for the reasons being fought over. Even if fully implemented Obamacare will still leave millions without health insurance. The reasons for this are not hard to discern. What we have now is a government that has become structurally and functionally obsolete and until this is addressed nothing of substance will change.

Ostensibly, congress exists to promote and protect their constituents' best interests but they do this only to the extent those interests are not in conflict with those of their financial backers - the "special interests" who are their true constituents, The fingerprints of these "special interests" are on virtually every piece of congressional legislation and this is the primary reason why our laws are so convoluted. There are endless examples I could point to and as I mentioned earlier, a prime example is the legislation creating the Medicare Part D Drug Program which prohibits government from negotiating prices on any of the drugs it buys. It also prevents the United States Patient-Centered Outcome Research Institute from considering price when evaluating drug effectiveness and it outlaws the importation of prescription drugs even though those drugs can save consumers up to 90% over domestic ones. How did Congress let this happen? The answer is the corrosive and corrupting influence of "special interests". In 2005 the pharmaceutical industry spent $250 million on lobbying Congress and that does not include the amount they spent on congressional campaign contributions. This amount dwarfs even what the defense industries spent on lobbying the Pentagon. Both Big Pharma and the defense industry spent these huge sums because they expect and get a substantial return on their investment and those returns come at the expense of us all, so clearly a new direction is needed to change both our governmental structure and our governance. To put this in perspective, John Friedman, an economics professor at Brown University calculated that over a ten-year period Big Pharma earned a profit on their investment of $242 billion. This makes investor Warren Buffett look like a piker. So it is the corrupting influence of "special interests" that is clearly the problem and they are aided and abetted, in this regard, by the divisiveness of the two party system.

1.4 - Campaign Finance Reform:

So the first issue we need to address is campaign finance reform which will marginalize these two culprits. Until and unless that is resolved none of my ensuing recommendations will have any meaning or effect, And doing this will have two very positive effects; one - it will eliminate the corrupting influence of "special interests" money and two - it will reorder our governmental structure away from one that is authoritarian, elitist, establishment and top down to one that is more inclusive, open and bottom up. To accomplish this we need to structurally change the Constitution and modify the first amendment guarantee of free speech to correct the Supreme Court's decision in "Citizens United". Specifically, we need to amend the Constitution to provide for direct governmental funding of all campaigns for federal office, i.e. the Congress, president and vice-president (hopefully the states would follow suit - they could also be included in the amendment but broadening it would lessen its chances of passage). Secondly, this amendment must outlaw all contributions from all other sources so that "special interests" influence is eliminated. Candidates must also be prohibited from using their own money to fund their campaigns which would prevent wealthier candidates from exerting undue influence (think Donald Trump and Michael Bloomberg). This would leave candidates and their campaigns free to focus solely on the issues at hand. A third provision to this amendment would prohibit public advocacy groups (political action committees - PACs) from naming, promoting or endorsing any candidate for public office. This includes any group that advocates for political, social, cultural, religious. economic, environmental or any other cause or outcome. These advocacy groups would still be free to comment and promote their positions on the issues. They could run radio or TV ads, publish blogs, host web sites, hold rallies and promote their cause in any other legal way. They would only be prohibited from endorsing, denigrating or associating themselves or their issues with any candidate or campaign. They would also be required to identify themselves, their membership and donor lists and disclose all their financial resources. This would level the playing field and inform the public of who or what are behind these groups and allow for better and more informed decisions. Individuals and the press would remain free to endorse or comment on any candidate or campaign. As it stands, these provisions would clearly be an infringement of the first amendment guarantee of freedom of speech, and preserving and maintaining free speech is an essential and fundamental right - but it is one that must to be balanced with necessity - and this right has its limits. As Justice Holmes said a century ago - one cannot go into a crowded theater and just yell fire. So a proper balance needs to be maintained and by allowing these groups to discuss their causes, but not endorse or interact directly with the candidates, strikes that balance.

Implementing this amendment will require an entirely new approach to the electoral process - one that will make the process more open and transparent. As things stand now, many of us feel that the game is "rigged" and to a great extent it is. In our two party system candidates emerge from a primary process where only party members can vote (this is not true in all cases and some states do allow cross-party voting in primaries but it is generally the rule). Republicans vote in their primaries and Democrats in theirs. There are no primaries for independents, yet independents comprise the largest bloc of voters, over 40% of the voting public. Yet come election day we are relegated to making a choice between candidates most had little choice in selecting, may not prefer and who may be only the least objectionable. This result is even more skewed in presidential elections were, due to the workings of the Electoral College, some states have more influence than others. This process limits our choices to card-carrying party members and inhibits otherwise qualified candidates from coming forward and engaging in the political process. As a result, the current makeup of Congress is heavily tilted toward lawyers which is unique in advanced democracies. Lawyers make up more than 50 percent of members in the Senate, and in the House that figure is about a third. Lawyers are not necessarily bad people (I am one) but engaging more people of all walks of life would broaden the views and opinions of our Congress and that diversity is what our founding fathers had envisioned. At our inception, neither they nor the Constitution perceived or foresaw the rise and dominance of the two-party system and the professional politician. A return to our roots is certainly in order.

Our current systems also means that candidates are beholden to the core ideals of their party and must tow the party line to gain financial support and be elected. Which leads to a second constraint in our present system. The day a candidate wins office is the day he or she must start to raise funds for the next campaign. Here is where the heavy hand of "special interests" tips the scales in our democracy. No candidate can succeed without this money, whether it comes through the regular party apparatus or directly into the candidate's campaign. And no "special interests" donor makes his or her donation without the expectation of special consideration for their cause. Tort lawyers donate to Democrats which is why Democrats continually block tort and medical malpractice reform, Evangelical Christians donate to the Republicans which is why they are so opposed to abortion and gay rights. There are practically no causes or issues that are not influenced by "special interests". The result is a Congress that is polarized, financially wasteful and gridlocked and this divisiveness is throwing sand into the gears of our democracy. Money is still the mother's milk of politics and the only way to clean up this mess is through this amendment. After which, money will still be the mother's milk of politics but at least it would be coming from our "mother' (the government). I also believe that creating more transparency in how our elections function will also provide stimulus for more public participation - by both voters and candidates. The limited number of Americans that now actually vote is a sad testament to how the public perceives the fairness of our democracy.

How this would be implemented and function in practice is open to several possibilities but however this issue is resolved, I believe the best way to serve the ends of democracy and make our government more open, expansive and inclusive is to get the public more directly involved in the process. This begins with how I propose we go about selecting our candidates. Each office would require a slightly different process but in the maln they would all start with interested people garnering support for their candidacy through a petition process; This would be an entirely different process to what we have now where we are essentially reduced to voting for candidates that have been preselected for us and are mostly professional politicos with questionable agendas and purpose. Again, these candidates are not necessarily bad or mal-intended people, they are just the wrong people and changing the composition of our elected representatives will change, for the better, the manner in which our democracy functions.

There is another aspect of the two-party system that merits discussion: that is the regimentation of political philosophy that this current system demands of its adherents. Political parties like to refer to themselves as "Big Tents", acceptant of a wide variety of diverse political views. The reality is otherwise. Party members may generally hold similar views but as individuals they vary in degree on specifics - agreeing on some issues and disagreeing on others. However, when it comes to voting on legislation they are all funneled into voting blocks which may not truly represent where each of them stands. But failure to conform to the party line, as dictated by its leaders, can lead to loss of key committee assignments and worse - financial and party support come election time. For example, during this past congressional budget standoff (October 2013) there were a sufficient number of Republican Congressmen that could have supported both a continuing funding resolution (to keep government open) and an extension of the borrowing ceiling (to avoid government default). They were prevented from doing so by the Speaker of the House because of pressure exerted on him by a small minority of very conservative Republican Congressmen (Tea Party adherents and their "special interests" supporters) who opposed any form of compromise. Yet, in various public interest polls a substantial majority of the public disagreed with the Republican stand and the ensuing governmental shut down - their wishes were ignored. This represents a shameful and blatant corruption of political power by a small minority intent on imposing their will on the majority and it is little wonder that the public's approval rating of Congress is now in single digits. The fact that this group ultimately gave in to the majority is small comfort and the damage they did is incalculable. This is not an isolated incident. As far back as 1919 the same kind of congressional obstruction occurred when a minority group of House members (then called the Irreconcilables) prevented a majority of Congress from affirming the Versailles Treaty which blocked American membership to the League of Nations. Claims that failure of American participation in that world body resulted in World War II are dubious, at best, but that the the majority was bested by the authoritarian minded minority are not. To resolve this we need to remove these Tents" - big, small or otherwise and replace them with a process that directly connects the public to their representatives without the interference or intervention of party hierarchy. As things stand now, political parties act as a funnel and gate keeper - standing between the people and their representatives - adding nothing to the equation and benefiting no one but themselves. The closer we can come to eliminating their unwarranted interference the more the public will be involved in the political process and the more open and responsive will be our democracy. This has nothing to do with Congress taking action that runs counter to public opinion. We elect our leaders to act on our behalf and in our best interest and sometimes doing the right thing runs against the grain. This is about political parties following the agendas of their "special interests" minders to the detriment of the people.

However, back to this amendment - there are two additional provisions that will be required to procedurally effectuate it. The first is a provision authorizing and requiring Congress to provide the funding and the second, to require that that funding be adequate enough to allow each candidate to reach and inform all voters in their respective districts of their position on the issues involved. Without this provision Congress would have an incentive to under fund the various primaries and general elections because it would benefit incumbents and restrict the reach and exposure of their opponents. Enforcing this second provision may require resort to the courts but by holding Congress to a standard of "funding adequacy" compliance can be assured.

The second would establish the mechanism for implementing this amendment. This provision also has two parts. The first is a provision for the creation and establishment of Election Oversight Committees. This provision would establish a standing committee for each election and each electoral district; i.e congressional and presidential. These committees would oversee the election process, dispense funds and validate the results. Each committee would be composed of five members who would choose a chairman from among themselves. The governor of each state would appoint the committee members for each congressional election. Committee members would serve at the discretion of the governor and could serve multiple terms. Congress would appoint the presidential election committee. However, no member of any of the committees could be a current office holder, an elected official or a government employee. This would insure that committee members were drawn from the public at large and be recognized civic leaders. The second part is the election process itself and this would also be a two step process. What I envision here is for primary and general elections similar to the current system but operating in a more open environment and unrestricted by the two party system. The existing parties would still be involved but would they would be reduced to the status of an advocacy group and no longer dominate the primaries or the process.

The process would begin with a series of primary elections that would replace the existing primary and caucus process for all federal offices. These would be followed by the general election so the system would mirror our current process, only the primary process would be different in that it would be open and totally devoid of party domination. This process would function somewhat differently for presidential elections where there would be an additional set of five regional presidential primaries preceding the general primaries. However, each starts in the same manner with prospective candidates circulating nominating petitions to support their candidacy (for presidential and vice presidential candidates the petition would be for a combined two-person slate). Petition supporters would be restricted to voters in the district covered by the office petitioned for. For presidential candidates that "district" would be one of five regional ones created by Congress for these primaries. These petitions would be validated by the Electoral Oversight Commissions and certify the number of signatures on each petition. The candidates with the most signatures would be certified to run in that primary. For the presidential primary, that would be the top five candidates in each of the five regional districts and for congressional primaries that would be the top ten candidates in each district (Fox News chose 10 as the right number for a Republican presidential debate in August 2015) . For congressional primaries, the two candidates with the most votes would face off in the general election in November. For presidential candidates the process would be the same except they would undergo an initial round of five regional primaries. For these primaries Congress would create five contiguous regions of equal population (or as nearly equal as possible). Hawaii would be deemed contiguous to California and Alaska contiguous to Washington State. The top two candidates in each region would advance to a national primary. Candidates could submit petitions in each of the five regional districts which means that the national presidential primary could potentially contain anywhere from two to ten candidates. The top two vote getters in the national primary would advance to the general presidential election. In all cases, an incumbent seeking re-election would automatically be included in the primaries without requiring a petition.

Implementing this amendment and the procedural changes it would mandate are best left to Congress - but a reasonable timeline for this process could be as follows:

All committees appointed by January 1st of
an election year,

All petitions submitted to the committees
one month later by February 1st of that year,

Committee validation and certification of
all candidates by March 1st of that year,

Regional Presidential primaries on the
first Tuesday of June of that year,

All primaries (congressional and
national presidential) on the first
Tuesday of September of that year, and

The General election on the first Tuesday
of November of that year.

A good example of how this concept could work is the
recent Boston, Massachusetts mayoral race (November
2013). It began in the prior spring when twelve candidates
declared for the office. During the summer each received

substantially equal coverage from the media and in particular the local public broadcasting stations (WGBH radio and TV) both sponsored several debates plus in-depth interviews and candidate profiles. Campaign funding was not equal but the differences between campaigns were not major. There was no discernable outside special interest money or influence involved and the candidates mostly focused on local issues - taxes, education, unemployment, income disparity, housing, and job creation. A primary was held in September with the top two vote getters - John Connolly and Marty Walsh advancing to the general election in November. During the ensuing two-month campaign there was very little negative advertising and what there was came from Connolly who charged that the Walsh campaign was receiving outside union support and money, but in the main they both mostly focused on local issues. In the general election Walsh prevailed by four percentage points in what was a spirited, clean and focused election. While this was a local affair centered on local issues it demonstrates how effective and transparent elections can be when "special interests" money and party domination are curtailed - though not entirely eliminated.

Standing in stark contrast to the Boston mayoral election was the November 2013 statewide election in New Jersey.

Governor Chris Christie was running for reelection and safely ahead in the polls. He eventually won reelection by a landslide with 60 percent of the vote. However, the real contest was for control of the legislature where, as reported in the New York Times, in a November 5th article, the heavy hand of outside "special interests" money intervened:

> "Democrats and unions, fearful of a landslide victory by Governor Chris Christie will reshape New Jersey's political
> landscape have poured tens of millions of dollars into a record-breaking outside spending campaign that has transformed the state's election season.

> The effort, intended to preserve Democrats dominance of the State Legislature and complicate Mr, Christie's plans to build a record of legislative achievement as he considers a presidential bid in 2016 has inundated some legislative districts with millions of dollars in negative ads on a scale never before seen in New Jersey.

> As of last Thursday, according to the state's election law enforcement board, outside spending for

candidates had topped $35 million, twice the amount
spent when Mr.
Christie, a Republican, was elected in 2009 and the
highest recorded by any state except California
(whose population is almost 8 times larger).

The surge of spending is likely to be replicated
around the country next year, as outside groups
from both parties signal
increasing interest in influencing state-level
contests".

What happened in New Jersey is not the exception it is the
rule and it is a scathing indictment of our present political
order. What it tells us is that both political parties put their
quest for power and rival dominance first and our national
well-being second. As this article points out, campaigns are
now spending obscene amounts of money on packaging,
marketing and selling candidates to voters and engaging in
negative and factually questionable advertising that
purposely masks and confuses the issues. The process is
aided and abetted by PACs that personally attack
candidates instead of the issues using, tactics that are no
different from those used by Madison Avenue to sell
breakfast cereal and, just like breakfast cereal, these

political equivalents are heavy on sugar and calories but mostly devoid of sustenance and nutrition. Resulting in incumbents spending way too much time campaigning and far too little performing their duties.

If we view this from a different perspective and draw a national graph of our political leanings we would see a voter distribution that looks something like a bell curve with the majority of voter opinions clustered around the center. What we get, in reality, is a graph where the center is hollowed out and the edges (one or two standard deviations left or right) are predominant and hold sway. This mismatch is directly attributable to the power of "special interests" money and party domination of the electoral process where it is mostly partisans who are the primary voters. What people desire in their representative and what they get is shaped by these forces and is not necessarily the same thing. As such, the present system stands as a gatekeeper and barrier between government and the people preventing a direct connection between the voter and his or her representative, You can think of this process as light distorted through a prism. The public's diverse political leanings are filtered and distorted by these prisms of "special interests" money and party dominance resulting in a government that is shielded and less responsive (sometime unresponsive) to their constituent's views. Leaving a public that is frustrated, alienated and less inclined to participate in the democratic process. So what I am proposing is what I believe is the most effective way to resolve our governmental structural impediments although certainly not the only way. However, what is essential and central to any governmental restructuring is the complete elimination of "special interests" money and a substantial reduction in party influence and power over the electoral process - especially in the primaries. Without these changes all others would, by comparison, be ineffective and at best cosmetic. In short, the current system of campaign finance and party domination are a cancer on our body politic and, if not surgically removed, the prognosis for a healthy democracy will be increasingly doubtful.

I am confident these changes will happen. I am less confident in predicting when. However, when I look back over the past two centuries I see a national will that was capable of making the necessary and significant structural changes as needs arose. Some of these were more substantial than what I am proposing (think of the abolition of slavery with the cost of over 700,00 lives and the enactment of universal suffrage which took 130 year) and they have been a positive force, encompassing a more expansive and inclusive democracy. But for all the progress our democracy has made we are still locked into the same top down authoritarian, elitist and establishment model that our founders created in 1787. In a sense we could call this "stage one" democracy model. What I am proposing would change this to a bottom up model that we could call "stage two" where the electorate and their representatives would have a singular connection, devoid of outside distortion or influence.

One final point - this amendment will also require a "Necessary and Proper" clause to allow Congress enough flexibility to legislate administrative rules for this process. For example, Congress could require that committees sponsor and hold two or three candidate debates for each primary and general election. They could also require the committees to compile and publish candidate position papers which could then be distributed to all voters in a printed form or be hosted on the committee's web site. The web site could contain the same information that is in the printed form plus video presentations by the candidates. Thus, this amendment would insure equal dissemination and exposure of each candidate and their positions. In a word - maximum transparency. The petition process would also have to be very tightly defined and regulated to prevent political parties and "special interests" groups from "gaming" the system. One way to accomplish this would be to have the committees control the petition process. They could initiate this by mailing a blank petition form to each registered voter in the district which would allow (empower) voters to nominate potential candidates themselves. By printing a unique control number on each form, the committees could insure that only one form is submitted per voter and since all signatures would, in any event, be vetted this would not raise privacy issues. Individuals, political parties and "special interests" groups would be free to run ads promoting their favored candidates but in this case it would be up to the voter to get the ball rolling. This, in essence, would be pure bottom up democracy in action.

1.5 - Gerrymander No More:

There are still more changes needed to improve our governmental structure and practices, and hence, our democracy. But I would be very hesitant to include or combine these others with this proposed amendment simply because the more involved amendments become the more opposition they attract and the prospects for enactment dims in proportion. So my next recommendations are better left for other amendments and other days but eventually these too must be addressed. One would put an end to the practice of gerrymandering and the other would eliminate the Electoral College. Neither of these has the magnitude or urgency of campaign finance reform or curtailing party dominance but they are both structural impediments to a more representative democracy and, in particular, ending gerrymandering would go a long way toward calming the contentious atmosphere and dysfunction of our the House of Representatives. Gerrymandering is a practice as old as the nation. It is the product of Elbridge Gerry who was a signer of the Declaration of Independence, a Revolutionary War envoy to France, a Governor and later a Congressman from Massachusetts. In order to enhance his reelection chances he had the state legislature reconfigure his district to include more favorable towns and exclude those less favorable. It worked very well and this practice has since been honed to a fine art by both parties. Every ten years congressional districts are redrawn by states legislative majority parties solely to create more favorable - i.e. safe -districts for their party. By definition, this also creates safe districts for the opposing party, but less of them. This results in legislatures that are contentious and less willing to bargain or compromise because this puts representatives at odds with their districts and invites primary challenges from more extreme opponents. The inability or willingness of moderate Republican congressmen to prevent the recent government shutdown is a perfect example. Further proof for this is that between 1964 and 2012 over 85% of all congressional house elections have been won by the incumbent party. This is an even more striking number when you consider that control of the various state legislatures have swung back and forth between the parties during this time frame. In California where the state legislature has been dominated by one party for decades the results are even more striking, Between 2002 and 2012 only one house seat changed affiliation in 265 elections. Not even the Soviets nor Cubans could boast of results like these.

The solution to this anti-democratic behavior is simply to de-politicize and automate the redistricting process. This fix can be accomplished through congressional legislation but the preferred method would be a constitutional amendment. This would be a better solution and make it impossible for Congress to change it in the future. A constitutional amendment would also forestall any judicial challenges that a legislative solution might invite.

The goal here is to devise a redistricting map that is equitable and as devoid of political intervention and manipulation as is humanly possible, This, I believe can be achieved by having an amendment that establishes specific selection criteria for redrawing district maps which will also insure the elimination of human bias. There are several metrics I could use to create this impartiality but the one I am proposing would require these committees (see below) to select a redistricting scheme that has the "shortest aggregate linear boundary measurements" from among all those proposed. A further proviso would require that no district contain a population differential that is more than a 1.05% or less than 95% of any other district. This would create districts that are concisely drawn and balanced and prevent the carve-outs that are so prevalent today. This sounds like a mouthful but in practice it merely means adding up the total linear boundary distances of all the proposed redrawn district schemes and selecting the one that has the least total linear boundary distance. For example if two maps were up for consideration and one totals 987,415.7 linear miles and the other 988,332.9 linear miles, the former would be certified as the new map because it has the shortest peripheral boundary measurement provided it can also satisfy the population distribution requirement.

As with campaign finance reform this would also be a two-step process, Step one would be for each state to create a redistricting oversight committee which would be appointed by its governor. Each committee would be composed of five members with the committee chairman selected from among them and, as with election oversight committees, be devoid of politicians and their associates. The governors would have 60 days from the final determination of census data and state district allocations to make the appointments or it would remand to the courts to make that determination. Once established, committees would invite the public, both individuals and groups to submit proposed redistricting schemes with a 60 or 90 day deadline for submissions. This would directly involve the public in the selection process as compared to what is now a closed door and opaque one. Each committee would then validate the boundary measurements of the various public submissions and declare the one that best meets the required criteria the winner. This may still result in districts that favor one political philosophy over another but the object here is not to homogenize the public's political leanings but rather to eliminate imbalances that are truly man-made and anti-democratic. I have no doubt that the outcome will substantially level the playing field and result in a Congress that is more congenial and less ideologically divided. There is another advantage to be gained in ending gerrymandering and that is in stemming the frustration and erosion of public confidence with the current system. The public is well aware that districts are drawn to political advantage and that knowledge lessens their confidence and participation in the electoral process. Only perceived fairness and transparency serve the ends of democracy and this amendment would go a long way toward achieving that goal.

The prospects for this proposal may seem far fetched but this problem is already under attack in a number of states including Iowa, Washington, Arizona, New Jersey, Idaho and New York. However, California has once again led the vanguard with recently passed legislation that took redistricting out of the hands of politicians and put it in the hands of a 14 member "citizens" board. The law opens board membership to any citizen who is not a current office holder, public official or immediate family member, lobbyist or large campaign donor. For the 2012 congressional election this citizen board re-drew the district map creating 53 new districts. In the following election there was a 26% turnover in the political affiliation of the state's congressional delegation. This is proof positive that reality based public participation in the electoral process is a winning strategy and solution to countering the corrosive effects of political party domination.

1.6 - Why the Electoral College?

My final proposed constitutional change would eliminate the Electoral College and replace it with direct popular election of the President and Vice-president. Initially, the Electoral College and state legislative appointment of Senators were a "safety valve" mechanism built into the Constitution by our founding fathers. Their purpose was to create a buffer between the voting public and high office by allowing "cooler heads" to prevail should the public err and vote in undesirable candidates for these offices. Their intent was for the House of Representatives to be the people's house similar to the House of Commons in England and its direct election was acceptable since the House was re-elected every two years and any misstep could be soon corrected. But the Senate and the executive offices were a different matter and here the founding fathers wanted to provide stability to the process by insulating them from direct public participation. They wanted the Senate to be a more stable institution like the British House of Lords and wanted that same stability for the executive office. This lack of faith and confidence in the public's ability to self-govern was the impetus for the Electoral College. Electors to the Electoral College were appointed by the various state legislators to insure that seasoned political actors could intervene if the public was carried away by fiery oratory and elected someone they deemed unsuitable. This veto power reserved for the Electoral College Electors was in many ways similar to the governmental process that exists in today's Iran. The elected Iranian government is free to pursue any policies it wishes so-long as they pass muster with the Ayatollah who, as the final arbiter, holds veto power. In concept, the Electoral College performs that same function.

Over time, as the two-party system gained traction, this Electoral College veto power diminished to where it is now almost non-existent (almost - although in theory it still exists). However, there is another negative and troubling aspect to this process (besides a buffered approach to electing our executive branch) and that is that the Electoral College may still elect a candidate who fails to win the popular vote. The first incidence of this occurred in the 1824 election. Initially Andrew Jackson won 90 electoral votes against John Quincy Adams' 84, but not a majority, so the election was decided by the House of Representatives. Again in 1876 when Samuel J. Tilden won the popular vote by 254,235 votes but in a compromise that freed the south from Reconstruction, the Electoral College elected the minority candidate, Rutherford B. Hayes, President. And in 1888 Grover Cleveland lost in the Electoral College to Benjamin Harrison but won the popular vote by 90,596 votes. More recently, in 2000, George W. Bush defeated Al Gore in the Electoral College (and shamefully also in the Supreme Court) but trailed Gore in the popular vote. Gore bested Bush by 543,895 in the popular vote. Had Gore been elected president by popular vote our recent history would have certainly been substantially different (think Iraq, waterboarding, global warming etc.).

Aside from this issue, the continued existence of the Electoral College belies a more fundamental flaw to our democratic process. And that flaw is the authoritarian, elitist, establishment and top down nature of our governmental structure which affects how our governance works. Early on it was not so detrimental and may, in fact, have been essential. But now it is not and clearly evident in the buffering of the Electoral College, in the arrogance of gerrymandering, the dominance of political parties, the overreach of "special interests" money and most recently in the senatorial rules change ruckus over filibuster closure regarding presidential appointments.

Historically the Senate had no rule or mechanism for closing off a senatorial filibuster. A rule for this was first adopted in 1917 allowing for closure with a vote of two-thirds of the Senate (66%). It was changed again in 1975 when the required closure vote was reduced to a three-fifths majority of Senators (60%) and that is where it has been until November 2013 when the rule was changed yet again to allow for closure with a simple majority vote (50%). What precipitated this latest Senate rules change was the inter-party animosity that has risen to the level of participant political warfare. To put this in perspective, in the past 224 years there have been a little over 200 presidential nominee filibusters. But more than half of these occurred during the past five years of Obama's presidency. What was a vetting process based on a candidate's credentials, capability and fitness for office has morphed into one of vetting based solely on political affiliation and, with no other discernible purpose, than to obstruct the president's agenda for partisan political gain. The roots of this dispute lie in the filibusters original purpose which was to provide the Senate with a safety valve mechanism for screening out appointees to administrative posts and federal judgeships. In actuality, it functions like a college fraternity's "black ball" rule where any fraternity brother can exclude a pledge and in the Senate any senator could derail a nomination. What was intended as a procedure for senatorial "advice and consent" of presidential nominations became in fact a requirement for senatorial unanimity. Over time the rules have been relaxed to where it's now functionally democratic. However, individual Senators still hold a level of veto power in a different rule which is the "Blue Slip" requirement that no nomination can go to committee if blocked by a home state Senator. While this filibuster dispute may seem only a parliamentarian rules battle, it is yet another symptom of a fundamental structural flaw in our governance and it raises the question of why a simple majority vote would not have sufficed in the first place. The answer to this harkens back to the founding fathers' distrust of direct democracy. For them the House of Representatives was the "boiling caldron" of public passion, while the Senate was the "cooling saucer" of reason and deliberation. The result of this thinking was a top down political philosophy of our founding fathers - which, in essence, was that those who govern know better than those that are governed. What has changed since then is not so much the structure of our governance as has the composition of the governed and that has changed beyond recognition. So we have arrived at a point in the evolution of our democracy where our governmental structure no longer functions - and this filibuster issue is just another manifestation of the many cracks in the wall.

1.7 - Top Down - Bottom UP:

Since the first caveman imposed his will on his neighbors, government has been structured as a top down authoritarian process. The words Chief, King, Emperor and Warlord are not terms normally associated wlth Compromise, Deference, Concession or Bipartisanship. Until the emergence of democratic government in England in the sixteenth and seventeenth centuries, autocracies were the rule and democracies had only existed briefly in Athens, Rome, and a few city-states and small countries like Geneva and Iceland. Until then, the vast majority of people had lived in autocracies. Some were benevolent but autocracies nonetheless. So what the founding fathers were faced with was devising a democratic form of government with little to guide them except their own colonial experience, what they could glean from England's constitutional monarchy and some historical examples which were short-lived and not terribly encouraging.

As a result, it's not surprising that what they devised was a government - democratic in principle - but heavily weighted toward the "establishment". This was, in many respects, an adaptation of England's constitutional monarchy where elected officials replaced hereditary ones along with the continuance of a separate and independent judiciary. For its time It was a bold departure from the past and a cautious and firm commitment toward self-reliance and self-governance. It established the first large modern democratic republic - but one with a limited franchise. The vast majority of people were excluded from participation. The percentage of eligible voters hardly made it into double digits and that meant that the reins of power remained in the hands of the wealthy, the educated and the propertied. Given the general public's level of political sophistication, education and financial stability anchoring the government in the hands of the establishment was, at the time, a reasoned approach. However, over the past two hundred years the landscape has changed in unimaginable and irreconcilable ways. The franchise is now open to almost everyone (but unfortunately not all), a high school education or better is now the norm, the philosophy of democracy is now deeply ingrained in our national psyche and we are prosperous almost beyond measure. But as the current political deadlock shows, we are chafing under a governmental structure designed for a different time and place. Fortunately, our basic governmental foundation is sound. Our constitution was wisely designed with change and adaptability in mind. There is no violent revolution required to right the ship - just a few constitutional amendments will suffice. But these changes will bring profound changes in our governing body and in our governance. Our government will still be peopled with some that are overly ambitious, egotistical and elitist but, hopefully, there will be more that are egalitarian. I think they will be more like our founding fathers who certainly had self interest in mind but balanced that with an overriding need to serve the common good. Back then being a congressman, senator or president was a public service not a lifetime career. And it is not just our governmental structure that is top down and out of sync, it is all aspects of our society as well. This approach to our societal organization is now a remnant of the past and due mostly if not entirely to technological and cultural limits of the times. News was delivered top down by newspapers, and radio and TV commentators. We are religious by nature and our morality and ethics were also administered top down from the pulpit to the people. Today our societal circumstances are substantially different. The Internet has fundamentally and irreparably changed that - there is now Facebook, Twitter and a host of other social media sites that have altered the way we interact with each other. Societal organization has gone "horizontal" from "vertical". As our society continues to evolve our government must also. So what I am calling 'bottom up" is nothing more than a change in orientation. By fine-tuning the Constitution I see our democracy becoming more open, expansive and inclusive. This in turn will lead to our representatives no longer being lawyer heavy but peopled with public spirited citizens of all stripes including educators, business, labor, professionals and others of all walks of life. Not only will our representatives be more diverse, their constituents will be as well and although political parties will still be with us there will be more of them and they will be vying for attention with each other and with other public interest groups (environmentalist, religious, social, etc.).

Once our leaders are freed from the yoke of party domination and undue "special interests" influence and pressure (think money) their focus will re-direct to issues where thoughtful, considered and reality-based solutions can be advanced and implemented. Going forward, there won't always be harmony and consensus, and differing views will still be contentious and strongly held. The pro life and pro choice groups will still be at each other's' throats. Conservatives will still decry big government and Liberals will want a more comprehensive safety net.   But I have no doubt that a Congress so constituted would never exempt Big Pharma from competition when feeding at the public trough.   Nor do I think it would extend tax breaks to the wealthy at the expense of the poor.   Rather, I believe a govemment derived from the people and vetted more directly by the people will be more rational, and this Is what I call bottom up where the impediments that separate the people from their representatives are dissolved and we move on to a more engaged and responsive democracy. And that would be a very good thing.

1.8 - What's Next? That Depends:

Predicting our future course is a perilous and often futile pursuit - one more prone to failure than success. So forecasting how a change in government structure will affect governance is at best speculation and my proposed constitutional changes may not automatically produce a more egalitarian or enlightened government. Our governmental structure is merely the tool we use to craft our democracy. How we employ that tool and the results it yields are a different matter entirely. In theory, a better tool should yield a better work product, and logic dictates that if our legislators are freed from the current shackles of "special interests" and political party dominance they should, by default, be more responsive to public sentiment. Ultimately, it is the public itself that has to define what are in its own best interest, and while I firmly believe that the broadest possible franchise (the wisdom of crowds) will yield the best governance, there are numerous historical examples where public opinion ran counter to its own best interest. This is not being negative, it is being realistic because the fact is that public opinion is not always based on facts or reality. Often our thinking is also colored by our personal prejudices, misconceptions, socioeconomic status, religious beliefs, political philosophy and unreasonable fears and ignorance - and sometimes just plain selfishness and greed. Add to this our cultural predisposition to Puritanism (which H. L, Mencken defined as "the unrelenting fear that somewhere someone may be happy") and you get results that can, at times, be self-serving, detrimental, be at the expense of others and in the end a benefit to no one.

Looking back over time it is hard to understand how we, our government and especially our courts allowed Jim Crow segregation of Black Americans to persist for almost a century. Especially in light of the Civil War constitutional amendments enacted specifically to prevent it. Or how, in World War II, we happily interned 120,000 Americans of Japanese descent (two-thirds of whom were citizens) merely for that reason, which was also a clear violation of their Constitutional guarantees. These policies not only tarnished our cherished beliefs in liberty and personal freedom they were divisive to our country. You might wonder how much greater our nation would now be if women and minorities had been allowed to fully participate in its growth and development at an earlier time. But in retrospect we can clearly see that in both cases public opinion and government action were driven by prejudice, ignorance and fear which masked reality and caused us to view these policies through a distorted lens. Apparently, humankind's capacity for self-deception is boundless and being introspective and viewing ourselves as we really are, is a near impossibility, both personally and as a nation and changing our governmental structure will do little to resolve that.

So, until our national social evolution and maturation process sheds these darker impulses and we base our policy decisions on firmer ground (facts and reality) we will continue in pursuing policies that are misguided and counterproductive. But if we take a step back and reflect on how our nation has progressed over time the outlook is not so dire. In fact, the good news is that the long term trend line is positive and improving at an accelerating rate. A good example of our improving governance is our government's handling of the latest financial disruption - The Great Recession. Especially when contrasted with what transpired with the last one - The Great Depression. Back in the 1930s economic theory and understanding were not as advanced as today and, like the study of medicine, was as much art as science. This lack of understanding led the Treasury and Federal Reserve to pursue policies that were mainly based on supposition and intuition and, as it turned out, the exact opposite of actions they should have taken. They tightened the money supply, reduced government spending and raised interest rates; all at a time when unemployment was skyrocketing, financial markets were in retreat and liquidity had evaporated. In the intervening decades economic research by John Maynard Keynes, Milton Friedman, Carmen Reinhart, Kenneth Rogoff, Ben Bernanke and a host of others has provided a much stronger understanding of just how financial markets function and they have laid out specific policies for dealing with them. This time around and armed with these new tools the Federal Reserve, Treasury and Congress attacked the Great Recession by recapitalizing the banking system (i.e. - government bailouts), lowered interest rates, expanded the money supply and stepped up government spending (stimulus - although on a limited basis). There are some that would argue against these policies but there is no question that these actions, taken in concert, averted a global financial disaster and in only a few years were responsible for turning our economy around.

While these two financial disruptions are not exact duplicates, their similarities are sufficient to show that actions based on empirically crafted economic theory can effectively repair an economy that has lost its equilibrium. When actions are not so based the outcomes can be more like what recently happened to the European Union (EU). Their response to the Great Recession (which was global) was to enact austerity measures which had the effect of contracting their economies. Their intent was to reduce budget deficits and strengthen their balance sheets but, instead, they only managed to reduce their gross domestic product which actually exacerbated them. The EU is only now coming out of its recession and, its unemployment rate is still considerably higher than ours.

As it was, the Great Depression lasted 10 years and may have gone on longer had it not been for the advent of World War II. Our Great Recession lasted only 3 years and while the recovery has been tepid It Is nonetheless a recovery. Our recovery has also been hampered by other global financial circumstances - like the continuing recession in the EU, a slowdown in the expansion of China's economy and the generally lethargic growth of the global economy.

As with all things political, our government's policies were not without criticism. The main ones being that stimulus spending does nothing to improve the economy - it only adds to the deficit - and only tax cuts can actually revive an economy. However, if we look at the facts underpinning these differing economic theories we can assess their validity based on their outcomes and separate reality from supposition. Unfortunately, economic theory is not an exact science but is instead distilled from different data sets, covering diverse economies and markets and often clouded by non-financial consideration that can intrude on the result. Still, over time and given enough data, a comfortable degree of certainty can be achieved about them. For example, saying increased demand and reduced supply will result in an increase in price is not as scientifically certain as saying water boils at 212 degrees Fahrenheit but it is widely accepted as an irrefutable fact. In the same way economic theory can be tested against the actions taken for accuracy.

However, one question you might ask is, if we now have all this great understanding of how economies and markets perform, how did the Great Recession occur in the first place? And the short answer is that being human we are prone to being optimists and all too willing to disregard or ignore signs we do not agree with or wish not to see. There certainly were a few who foresaw the financial crisis but their voices were drowned out by the majority who saw the continued increase in housing prices and the robust economy as proof that they were wrong. Humans are much better in dealing with what is than what may or will be (global warming anyone?). So until the housing market imploded and we had an actual financial disaster on our hands there was no impetus to change course. This optimism was also supported by the long-held belief that while local housing markets occasionally experienced downturns, that had never happened nationally (except during the Great Depression and that was considered an anomaly).

As it turned out the collapse of the housing market was not localized and it threatened the entire economy just as the collapse of the capital markets dld in 1929. Fortunately, the response this time was based on economic theory and data that was not then available. For starters, immediate action was taken that focused on returning to a normal level of market liquidity and restoring economic activity which included growing the gross domestic product, achieving housing price stability and above all a renewal of consumer confidence. Without these actions people would hoard what money they had, slash their spending and the economy would have slowly bound up. But this goal could not be achieved through policy changes alone, it had to be accompanied by a heavy dose of monetary muscle to prime the pump and get the economy up and running again. And there were only three economic engines that had the capacity and resources to accomplish that. One - the Private Sector; Two - State and Local Government; and Three the Federal Government. To evaluate what was actually done against what the critics say should have been done one needs only to look at how each engine performed and gauge the results . While this exercise is more nuanced than a purely scientific one, it will, in the end, separate facts and reality from fiction and speculation.

One - The Private Sector: Back in 2007 and 2008, when subprime mortgages hit the fan, so to speak, the entire domestic economy started to buckle. After Bear Stearns and Lehman Brothers collapsed it spread to encompass and threaten the entire global financial structure. In an environment like that the private sector was just not structured or capable of providing the needed support. The private sector is market driven and self-centered - not egalitarian by nature - and when the markets contracted their concerted reaction was to cut expenses, layoff employees, slash salaries, reduce inventory, husband cash and shutter marginal operations. Any CEO who ignored this course of action would soon be counted among the unemployed. Unfortunately, none of these actions helps to rejuvenate an economy and they are collectively the polar opposite of what was needed. So while the resources were, there the will was missing. Between 2007 and 2013 the private sector managed to squirrel away almost two trillion dollars and then sat on it waiting for a recovery to begin. Cutting taxes would have only added to this hoard. And what some corporations actually did with this this money was not to invest it their business but to buy back their public shares - which did absolutely nothing to restore the economy.

Business in general and big business in particular is not prone to take chances and will only embark on programs of investment and expansion when they are reasonably certain of a significant return on their investment (Return on Investment - ROI). As such, their actions are a lagging indicator of economic activity and recovery. They often delay hiring and increased production until they absolutely have to. While good times lead to corporate bloat, bad times lead to near starvation. So in and of themselves the private sector could not contribute much to a turn-around. What government critics will argue is that If corporate taxes had been cut the private sector, by itself and un-prodded, would have embarked on a program of investment and expansion. This is just plain false. All that tax cuts would have accomplished is to have increased their already hefty nest egg. Corporate taxes whether high or low are only one element the private sector considers when evaluating investment and expansion. The more critical elements are opportunity, market potential and demand, resource availability (including capital, material and human) and competition. When these are all factored together, business calculates the result against their expected return - their ROI. And If that potential ROI is high enough they move forward and if not they stay pat. Certainly there were enough financial resources already in place without the additional stimulus of a tax cut and, even if taxes had been cut to zero, business would not invest or expand until it is satisfied about its ROI. Through the recession, business remained constrained and on the sidelines as a non-starter.

Two - State and Local Govemment: The second available source for stemming recessionary tides are, collectively, state and local governments. However, a common element of their governmental structure is their inability to run budget deficits. They can float long term debt through bonds but they cannot incur negative current account operating budgets. Without that capability their resources are minimal and constrained. During a recession, their revenue, from taxes and fees of all stripes (property, income, excise, etc.) are substantially reduced. Faced with diminished revenue, state and local governments have little choice but to circle the wagons and cut expenditures. Salaries are cut, employees laid off (including teachers, firemen and police) and infrastructure projects curtailed with the predictable result of substantially increased unemployment. Welfare and social service assistance are also reduced just at the time when needed most. The only two alternatives to circumvent these depressive results are to raise taxes to increase revenue which in a recession is politically suicidal or to tap into a "rainy day fund", but these funds rarely exist since politicians, like children, can't keep their hands out of the cookie jar. So rather than being a source of recovery, state and local governments, through their economic contractions and lack of foresight, serve only to exacerbate it.

Three - The Federal Government: With the private sector voluntarily sidelined and state and local governments constrained by their budgetary borrowing limitations the only remaining viable recession fighting resources was the Federal Government (including the Federal Reserve - collectively the Fed). Fortunately, the Fed has several powerful weapons at its disposal with the main ones being its ability to print money and incur budget deficits. This allows it to step in and enact programs that pump money into the economy and create economic activity where none exists or, as T. S. Eliot might have put it, "'to breath life into the dead land''.

The basic thinking behind stimulus policy is that if government can get money into the hands of those who need it most they will, in turn, spend most of it on goods and services. This will stimulate and revive the economy, prodding the private sector to hire employees and make capital investments, thus restoring the economy back to health and ending the recession. Needless to say, there are differing opinions as to the effectiveness of thls philosophy. These various opinions while they are not monolithic generally fall into one of two competing camps. At the risk of oversimplification - stimulus supporters are economically Keynesian and politically Democrat while those against are "Austrian School" economically and politically Republican or Libertarian. Stimulus itself is a generic and plastic concept - it can mean many things such as direct government spending on unemployment assistance and infrastructure projects and it can also be accomplished through monetary policy intervention by lowering interest rates, expanding the money supply and cutting taxes. Stimulus, by its nature, is expensive and requires spending more than you have. As individuals, we do this when we tap into our home equity lines or credit cards and when our government does it they borrow by selling bonds and increasing the national debt. The other side of the "stimulus" coin (the Austrian side) is austerity which is contractive and requires reducing expenditure to match income, and that is exactly what state and local governments were forced into due to their budgetary structures.

The outcomes of these various policies are somewhat imprecise and will always be subject to partisan debate. But that does not mean that their effects cannot be determined and assessed. To do this we must first start by determining their effectiveness in comparison to competing policies. The easiest of these to compare is stimulus to austerity. In recovering from the last recession (the Great Recession) America relied on several approaches to stimulus while the Europe Union (EU) resorted primarily on austerity. The results of each policy are clear and unambiguous. The EU is just now coming out of its recession and with an unemployment rate that is still in double digits, especially among their youth. America, on the other hand, has been out of recession for several years. Our gross domestic product (GDP) is not quite back to where it was but, again, when compared to the EU's we are considerably improved. And while our unemployment rate is somewhat high by historical standards it is significantly better than the EU rate (there may be a structural change taking place in the economy which is keeping unemployment higher than would normally be the case this far into the recovery, but I will touch on that in Book ii). So in terms of this latest recession, stimulus policy has clearly proven to be the better approach, although the results could have been better had stimulus been employed to a greater extent than it was.

One issue that clouds this comparison is the differing governmental structures between American and the EU. We have a federal government that can speak with a single voice (when it so desires) whereas the EU is a confederation of separate and sovereign nations (think of our first form of government - The Articles of Confederation). So while the Fed can take action that binds the whole, the EU can't - at least not without first getting member ratification. Our Federal Reserve and the European Central Bank (ECB) are also structured differently and I don't want to get to far off track but the EU's ability to affect their respective economies are also different and for the same reason - a lack of authority to act timely. Had the ECB intervened earlier, the depth of their recession might have been mitigated, but as it was it took far too long for the member nations to recognize the danger or respond to it. By contrast the Fed acted quickly. Congress passed a 780 billion dollar direct spending stimulus package while the Treasury and Federal Reserve intervened in the banking system (bailing out the banks) and saving AIG, Freddie Mac, Fannie Mae, Chrysler and General Motors from falling. While there has been much criticism of this intervention I shudder to think what the result would have been had these actions not been taken place - and taken promptly. The fact remains that the government recovered almost all of its "investment" so while it was a bailout in the end it was not a handout.   And as for AIG - the government actually made a substantial profit.

A second issue for the EU Is that stimulus requires spending more than you have but to do that you have to have the capacity to borrow and for the EU that was problematic. Because of the EU's governmental structure, the recession was not of universal effect but was mainly centered in only five countries which have become more commonly referred to as the PIIGS (Portugal, Ireland, Italy, Greece and Spain). Each of these countries stands on its own in a confederation.   With their borrowing ability depending solely on their own creditworthiness and not on the EU's, as a whole. Since each of these countries already had massive debt, their ability to borrow more was severely constrained.

Due to their structural differences and circumstances America and the EU took different paths to recovery. However the EU could have and ultimately did intervene to stabilize the PIIGS's monetary condition, and that helped, but austerity remained the EU's primary policy and the results of that shows, as with the Great Depression, that that policy is not effective. With Greece in particular, austerity caused their GDP to plunge and, while it did cut Greece's overall debt, its GDP plunged even further with the result that the ratio of debt to GDP actually increased while unemployment remains above twenty percent. So while the EU, as a whole, is coming out of the recession that is little comfort for the people of Greece for whom the struggle continues.

The other comparison that can be made is to the effectiveness of various stimulus policies as compared to each other. As for monetary policy there is little debate. Monetary stimulus is far more effective than belt tightening austerity and this was proven this last time around when the Federal Reserve and Treasury quickly used it to effectuate recovery. The Milton Friedman school of economics may have taken a slightly different policy approach to this but would not have disagreed with either the purpose or result.

Where different opinions do still exist Is in the area of direct government intervention and, as this requires both massive borrowing and spending, the arguments here are more political than economic. The politics are that Republicans believe tax cuts are the most effective direct economic stimulus and the best way to keep government small. While Democrats favor direct spending which, by its nature, is expansive and generally leads to a larger governmental footprint. However, putting aside this question of whether an engaged govemment need also be a big government, the answer to the question of which direct stimulus is most effective is also clear and conclusive,

Numerous economic studies have shown that tax cuts, at best, create no more than a one-to-one relationship when measuring the velocity of money in the economy. Velocity, in economic terms, means the number of times money turns over or spreads through the economy. If a person receives a dollar from someone and spends it on some goods or services, the velocity of that dollar is one. If the recipient of that dollar, in turn, spends it on goods or services with someone else, the dollar has then change hands twice and the velocity is now two. As money flows through the economy it stimulates it - the greater the velocity the greater the stimulus. With tax cuts the vast majority of money injected into the economy goes into savings and stops there. And while savings are generally a good thing - they are not during a recession. Therefore, tax cuts do little to stimulate the economy. On the other hand, programs like food stamps, unemployment benefits and infrastructure construction projects keep the money flowing and velocity high. For food stamps and unemployment benefits that velocity is about 1.7% to 1.8% and represent a much greater benefit from stimulus than do tax cuts.

So, if the facts are clear and we know which stimulus policies work and which ones don't, why then doesn't government just rely on these kinds of direct assistance programs to revitalize the economy, end the recession and just forget-about tax cuts? The answer is quite simple - "special interests". The people who benefit the most from tax cuts are the people who also fund election campaigns and It is not just stimulus policy that these "special interests" affect. There are an endless list of measures that government (Congress and state legislatures) support which, in the bright light of day, could not pass the sniff test but they are continually enacted because they benefit one "special interests" group or another. The reality is that government knows what the facts are; it knows the correct policies to apply to these facts; but it doesn't because the legislative process is derailed by the intervention of various "special interests" seeking personal gain over the greater good. So the solution to this problem is seemingly straightforward, We need to put a stake in the heart of "special interests". While that may seem a bit severe the point is that we have a governmental structure that is dominated by these "special interests" groups and until we separate them from the electoral process and un-encumber our representatives from their undue influence we will never get out from under this rock. I am not saying that "special interests" have to be completely vanquished or eliminated. What I am saying is that their power must be reduced to the point where it is balanced with everyone else's interest in petitioning government and electing representatives. They can still have a seat at the table. Just not at the head of the table, and that is equally true of political parties as well.

Accomplishing this is going to be difficult but not impossible and it starts with changing our governmental structure. The number one change, by far, is going to be a constitutional amendment that reforms campaign finance and eliminates the power of "special interests" and to a lesser degree political party dominance. Secondly, we need to eliminate gerrymandering, and finally, the Electoral College.

I have not doubt that these changes will happen. The long arch of history shows that we are steadily, if not evenly, making progress toward expanding our democratic footprint and becoming a more expansive and inclusive democracy.

Certainly the abolition of slavery and the expansion of the franchise to women were more contentious and daunting than what I am proposing.   I would put this effort on an even footing with the constitutional change that established direct election of senators which only changed the structure of government, not its function.   You could argue that governmental function was also altered but since political parties continued to dominate the process I think the change was mostly structural.

There is another reason for my optimism - one that is somewhat more intuitive than factual. Since our earliest days, organized government, whether dictatorial or democratic, has always been a top down affair. Democracy has only made it seem less so. In theory, we get to elect our leaders. But in actuality our leaders are pre-vetted and selected for us by political parties and their bosses. So the process remains essentially top down and perverted by "special interests" money. There is an old adage that goes "we have the" best government money can buy" - but unfortunately it's no joke. Political bosses and backroom deals have always been part of the political process but so has compromise and cross-aisle cooperation. Over the past 20 to 25 years this process has been substantially replaced with a gerrymandering system of fortified districts separated by a "no man's land" where reaching across the aisle is no longer an option. Our democratic process is not working and our country is increasingly disillusioned and dissatisfied with our choices and leaders - our government has become polarized and bound up, This became more apparent after the Supreme Court decision in Citizens United unleashed a flood of "special interests" money into the political process. As a result, I sense we are approaching a tipping point similar to that of the Progressive Movement of the early 1900s. Back then, corporate abuse and corruption became so evident that it created a public backlash. The same level of discontent is now afoot in the land, and properly channeled and orchestrated, could lead to a change in our governmental structure. And this time around this change could actually alter our governmental process from top down to bottom up. Change won't happen by itself - It will require direction and focus - but now both the times and the climate are ripe.

1.9 - A Coalition of One:

There are a number of ways that these constitutional amendments could be effectuated. At one end of the spectrum would be a frontal assault. Possibly Warren

Buffett, Bill Gates, George Soros or some others could be persuaded to donate a ton of money to the cause and finance a legion of lobbyists to directly attack Congress on behalf of these amendments (only one at a time and starting with campaign finance reform). But I think a better approach would be to follow the example of the Anti-Saloon League (ASL) successful campaign that enacted the Nineteenth Amendment to the Constitution (the Volstead Act - better known as Prohibition).

The fight for a constitutional amendment to banish alcohol from the American landscape was a simmering political issue for almost fifty years. As far back as the 1870s the Woman's Christian Temperance Union (WCTU) had mobilized thousands of women to protest and lobby for its enactment. But the WCTU had a broad and diverse agenda and diluted its efforts with a host of other social issues including women's suffrage and child labor law reform. In 1893 a new organization, the Anti-Saloon League, was formed to further the cause but with the sole purpose of enacting prohibition. During their 20 year campaign they often allied themselves with numerous like-minded groups but only to the extent that it furthered their cause. Their most effective weapon was in organizing coalitions of voters in each congressional district that voted as a block for the candidate that supported prohibition - in essence, a single issue constituency. If both candidates support the amendment the coalition was free to vote its conscience, but if not, their support went solely to the candidate that supported prohibition - forming a coalition of one.

I think a similar strategy could be used here but it would need to be updated to reflect the current state of technology and social organization. The ASL and their partners were focused first on electing a Congress that would support their cause and secondly, on the language and form of the amendment. I would approach this in reverse order starting with drafting a proposed amendment first and then soliciting congressional support. But aside from this difference I believe the ASL experience shows a plausible way to accomplish this goal.

However it is important to understand the depth of the problem we face. In the 2014 congressional elections there were 435 house and 36 senate seats in contention (of which 3 were to fill unexpired senate vacancies). Of these, 32 house seats and 8 senate seats were decided by 10 percent or less of the votes cast between the major candidates (not including third-party candidates). In addition, there were 32 house seats and one senate seat that were uncontested. The rest were clearly landslides with many decided by more than a 50 percent vote difference. It is no wonder that we have a Congress that is completely ideologically divided, polarized and gridlocked. And it is hard to believe that if the elections were not controlled by "special interests" money and party domination that one state and 32 congressional district could not have come up with more viable alternative candidates.

1.10 - So What's the Plan? :

What follows is both a workable and plausible plan, but keep in mind Clausewitz's observation that battle plans are only valid until the first shot is fired. However, you have to start somewhere so I would begin by seeking out a core group of like-minded individuals to join together to form a core management team to lead the charge. There are numerous groups already striving to achieve this goal and finding a few dedicated and energized fellow travelers should not be that hard, especially in this age of the Internet, blogs and social media.

While I am obviously very interested in seeing this happen I also have a proven track record of managerial ineptitude and my active inclusion could only serve to slow things down. So instead, I would prefer the role of Observer / Advocate and leave the field of battle to those more qualified. We would also have to brand our effort and my recomendation would be for "thewedge.org" which, to me, symboliies the thrust of where we are going and how we can get there. This team's next step would be to recruit a committee of ten or fifteen major university constitutional law professors to draft a proposed amendment along the lines outlined above. I think creating a draft amendment is an essential and vital first step. It provides specificity and details to exactly what our goal is and it preemptively sidelines vague and competing strategies. And by having the proposed amendment crafted by a distinguished committee of constitutional law professors it adds authority and respectability to the cause.

Armed with a draft amendment we could reach out to all the existing like-minded groups with the intent of bringing focus along the lines used by the ASL in forming their coalition of one. In essence, these other groups would have to either join our effort and adopt our proposed amendment or go their own way. This may sound undemocratic or overly harsh - my way or the highway - but having different groups, each sporting their own vislon won't work. It will dilute the effort and, in the end, we will fail to achieve our goal. Having a draft amendment would also put Congress on notice as to what we want enacted. By way of example, Grover Norquist followed a similar strategy wlth hls "no new taxes" pledge and with it was able to successfully extract commitments from numerous members of Congress. Hls policy was clearly articulated and sharply defined. You either signed and accepted his pledge completely or he would retaliate and marshal his forces against you. Our strategy should be similar and our wedge just as sharp.

After our coalition is in place our next step would be to build a field organization - one in each of the 435 congressional districts. We could do this by recruiting students and faculty from colleges and universities located in or near each district. Thls may require some funding to compensate for time and expense but let's skip over these details for now. Once we have a credible organization in place, raising money should not be that difficult. I am also working on the assumption that these field organizations would form the bases from which we could reach out to communal groups for support and to weld together a cohesive strategy and meaningful single purpose voting block. How successful this strategy will be is dependent on a number of factors. One is how competitive the various congressional races are and how willing incumbents will be to sign on to our amendment. The first may be the most daunting since in the 2014 Congressional election only 7 percent of house races and 25 percent of senatorial races could really be called competitive and that is using a very liberal definition of competitive. However, even if the general election is not competitive the preceding primaries may be, so there may be more lift here than first appears. There is also the issue that any candidate that takes a position against campaign finance reform is taking a negative position and leaving themselves open to attack on that point. Just as no candidate stumps for tax increases, being against campaign finance reform is not a winning strategy. The ASL had the moral high ground and was able to pull together voting blocks of significant size - from ten to twenty percent of registered voters so their coercive power was tremendous. But even a smaller voting block can be intimidating and persuasive as Grover Norquist has successfully demonstrated.

The second point is that many incumbents may actually be in favor of this amendment. Since they would automatically be included in the first round primaries they would have a significant advantage over their rivals. As things stand now, incumbents are often challenged by extremist party members on the left and right and an open non-partisan primary would allow them to be more forthright in their positions, less threatened by the fringe and leave the public better informed. More importantly, this amendment would free them from "special interests" pressure. I can't imagine that there are actually congressmen or senators who truly enjoy having their chain jerked every time "special interests" are in play or that spending a substantial majority of their time on fundraising is appealing. So incumbents may find this amendment quite liberating. Once campaign finance reform is achieved we can move on to the other amendments - gerrymandering and the Electoral College. These should be more easily achieved once we have a less partisan Congress and with gerrymandering there may actually be another route to the summit - a judicial one. On June 29, 2015 the US Supreme Court, in Arizona State Legislature v. Arizona Redistricting Commission, et al, declared as legal a commission that Arizona voters had created through a ballot initiative to remove redistricting from the hands of state legislators. Like California this ends gerrymandering in their state. The more this happens the greater the potential of passing a constitutional amendment on campaign finance reform.

1.11 - The Spastic Cat and Other Fantasies:

Democracy is not monolithic and by its very nature, is a process of compromise by competing interests. Each of these interests is also, by nature, striven to be dominant and hold sway over others. Since the dawn of our nation that dominance has been the providence of the establishment - predominantly White Anglo Saxon Protestants (WASPS) but always the wealthy, the educated and the propertied and always exercised to the exclusion of the Others - who were variously Blacks, Hispanics, Asians, Jews, Catholics, Irish, Southern and Eastern European, women, the poor and the disadvantaged.

Initially that dominance was exercised by limiting the franchise exclusively to the establishment. However, over time, and in theory, the franchise has expanded and now almost all citizens have a right to vote. But while out-and-out prohibition has been curtailed all restrictions have not been entirely eliminated. Recently, a group of states (predominantly southern conservatives) have enacted voting rights laws ostensibly to curb voting fraud by requiring additional proof of citizenship. This is, at best, a solution in search of a problem. It is, in reality, a thinly-masked attempt to limit the franchise and marginalize minority voters. In the end, I think this effort will fall to judicial scrutiny. In the past, poll taxes and weighted voting were also employed for this same mission. Those and other attempts a marginalization have since been discredited and eliminated by the Voting Rights Act of 1973 and the Supreme Court Decisions in Baker v. Carr (1962) and Wesberry v. Sanders (1964) thus leaving gerrymandering as the last bastion of establishment bias and dominance. These two landmark cases established the concept of "one man one vote" but the courts have since stumbled in applying this concept in evaluating various legislative redistricting plans, with courts straddling a knife-edge in determining whether plans are intentionally discriminatory or are justifiable exercises of the legislative prerogative. In essence, the courts have said that they will act where discriminatory intent is clear but will not substitute their judgment for that of the legislatures where it is not.

But where that line should be drawn has been evolving. That districts must contain equal (or as equal as possible) numbers of voters was established fifty years ago in Baker v. Carr, but the validity of the racial, ethnic or political makeup of equally sized districts was not. And the question that raises is this - if a district, equal in size, is drawn so as to minimize a particular group, does that, per se, violate the fourteenth amendment equal protection clause and the fifth amendment equal protection guarantee? The answer is, not necessarily. It depends on discerning legislative intent and certainly there will always be districts with clusters of minority voters so the question is really one of are those clusters happenstance or are they intentionally arrived at? And that intent can be inferred by the geographic structure of the district. If a district's geographic contours vaguely resembles the silhouette of an cat that has gotten its tale caught into an electrical outlet or if it looks like the curve outlines of a meandering river its prejudicial intent is pretty clear. But if a district is drawn with economy and no discernible attempt Is shown to carve out or isolate minority groups the courts should not and will not disturb the legislative prerogative,

I would still prefer my constitutional amendment over judicial intervention. But not being greedy - if the courts move more aggressively and apply strict oversight to the legislative process a similar result may be had. In the past the courts have been reluctant to substitute their wisdom for that of the legislatures but as demographics of redistricting are becoming clearer the willingness of courts to intervene has become more likely. Comfort for thls can be found in Cox v. Larios (2004 where Justice Stevens said "I remain convinced that in time the present failure of judicial will will be replaced by stern condemnation of partisan gerrymandering". We can only hope.

1.12 - Hope, Faith and Caution:

In the final analysis, my proposals may not play out exactly as intended but I do think they will occur in a substantially similar form and that this will happen sooner than later. In the short history of our republic we have made great strides in opening and expanding our democracy, but in a very real sense we are still a "Phase One" democracy. One that is structured to ensure the dominance of a top down authoritarian, elitist, establishment governance. By enacting these changes we can transform and elevate our democracy to "Phase Two" - one that is bottom up and one that establishes a direct connection between the people and their representatives. Once we have achieved this goal we can move on to clean up and dismantle the web of "special interests" laws and regulations that are perverting our democracy. And with a more balanced and open governmental structure we can turn our attention to how government can be more responsive to all our needs and how it can create a more inviting environment to grow and strengthen our democracy. This I will endeavor to do in Book II.

However, a word of caution is in order. Predicting the future or how change will play out is a dicey business. When prohibition was being considered there were many who saw a utopian world ahead. Poverty would be eliminated and domestic violence and family discord would disappear - in a nutshell the nation would become content and happy. Only a few foresaw the rise of organized crime or the blatant corruption it engendered. Fewer still understood that the ability of government to enforce its laws depends greatly on the willingness of the people to be governed. Judging by the failure of our "fifty year war on drugs" it's a lesson yet to be learn.

But there is a difference. What I am proposing is not to limit or regulate societal conduct but rather to open and expand our governance to be more inclusive, expansive and responsive to society, i.e, the people. So with that end in mind I remain cautiously optimistic that our best days lie ahead but it will be up to all of us to see that happen.

2.1 - Epilogue:

In his excellently researched and written book "America's Bitter Pill", Steven Brill relates the story of our government's efforts at reforming our broken healthcare system. In part, he sights a healthcare summit that then Montana Senator Max Baucus convened in June of 2009, with the intent of finding consensus among the 300 or so assembled major players, including Big Pharma, hospitals, medical device manufacturers, medical insurance companies and healthcare providers. In his opening remarks Baucus' concerns and reservations are clearly evident.

> "Some people suggest that because the American system is so complex and because it is so tied to political pressure (think "special interests") in all different segments, whether it be pharmaceuticals, insurance companies, consumers of health care, and whatnot, that perhaps we should look to some kind of a Federal health board, somewhat patterned after the Federal Reserve system, to help solve some of these problems"

What Baucus was alluding to was the base closing commissions (Defense Base Closure and Realignment Commission - BRAC) used by Congress in 1990 to ease constituent pressure on individual congressmen who were directly affected by these base closings. This commission independently developed a list of bases to be closed and submitted it to Congress which could only accept or reject the list but not modify it. This helped shielded individual congressional members from direct responsibility for local base closures.

However, there is a very large political distinction between using this kind of commission for base closures and also for healthcare reform. And that distinction is that while closing bases had a direct and negative effect on local businesses and communities it did not have any effect on "special interests". The military industrial complex sold just as many tanks, guns and planes to the government after the closings as before so they were not financially affected and as such they were not part of the problem or its solution. And while local interests can bring a lot of heat on a congressional member it doesn't compare to the heat that "special interests" can generate.

This is why this type of commission was never created for healthcare - because the "special interests" simply would not have allowed for it and because "special interests" did not need it to get the carve outs they sought and won in the final bill. As a result, the net effect of Obamacare is that costs are not reduced at anywhere near what they could have been if "special interests" had been sidelined.

Coverage is also not as broad as it could or should be but that has more to do with political considerations and those considerations are also compounded and skewed by our governmental structure and its effect of our existing governance.

So, if we hope to reform our governmental structure and move from a Phase One democracy that is top down, elitist, establishment and authoritarian to a Phase Two democracy that is bottom up, egalitarian and more responsive to the people's needs there are two things we must recognize and respond to.

The first is that we cannot rely on our current elected officials to achieve any meaningful reform because they are a product of the system and as such are totally and completely incapable of reforming our government from the inside. Baucus made that clear in his opening remarks.

The second is that since our government is not going to voluntarily reform itself - it will be completely up to us - *we the people* - to see that that happens. Therefore, we must create an organization that is separate and apart from government. To help further this along I have created a comment section to my Blog (ampu-form.org) to provide a meeting place where comments, opinions and discussion can take place and hopefully where an organization can develop that will see us through to a better America.

www.ingramcontent.com/pod-product-compliance
Lightning Source LLC
Chambersburg PA
CBHW062011280526

45787CB00005B/2067